Copyright ©2020

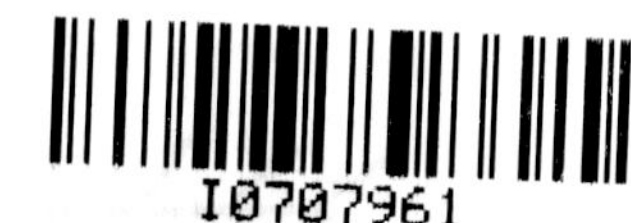

ALPHABET

Coloring Book
For Kids

This Book

Belongs To

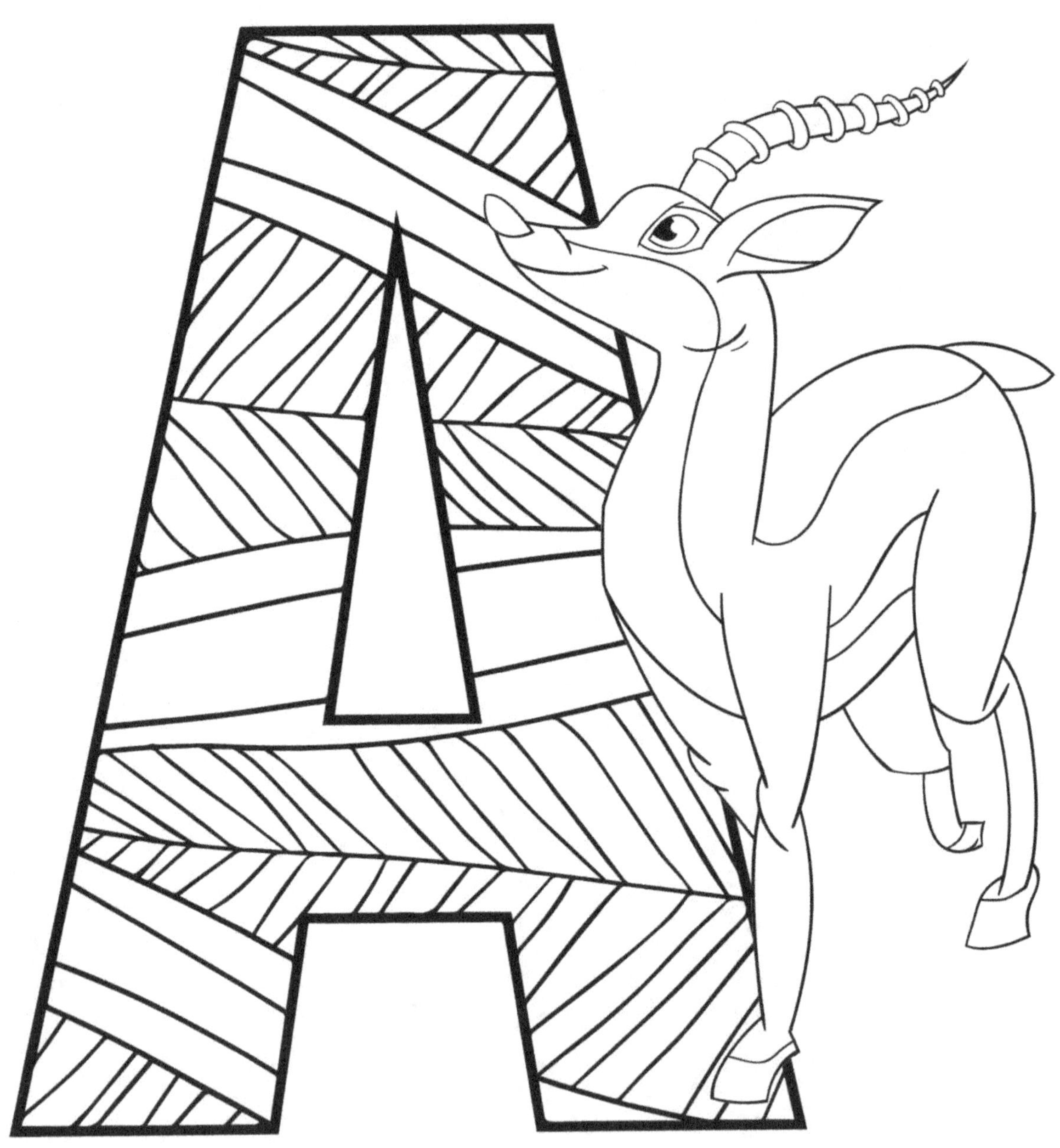

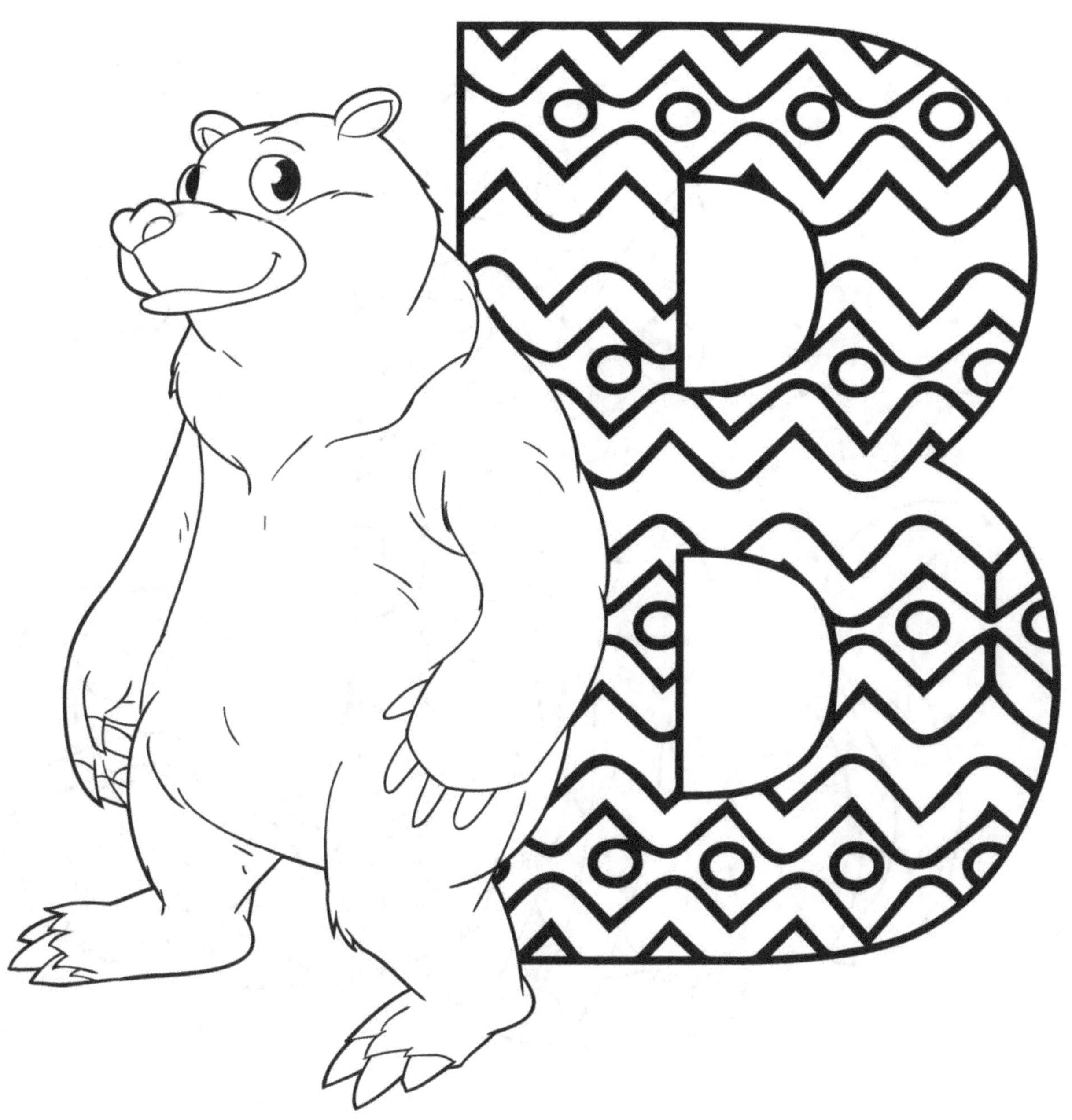

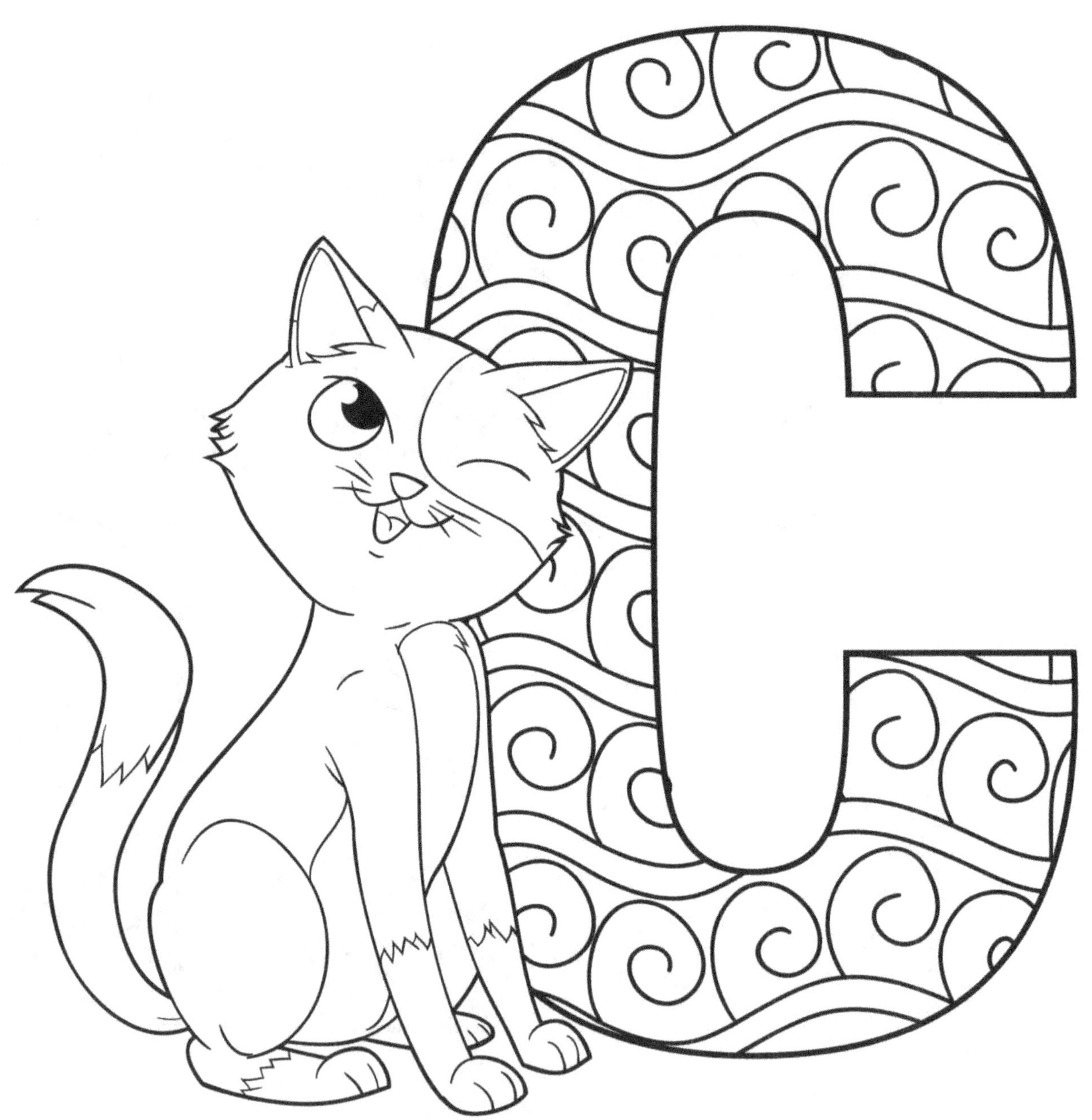

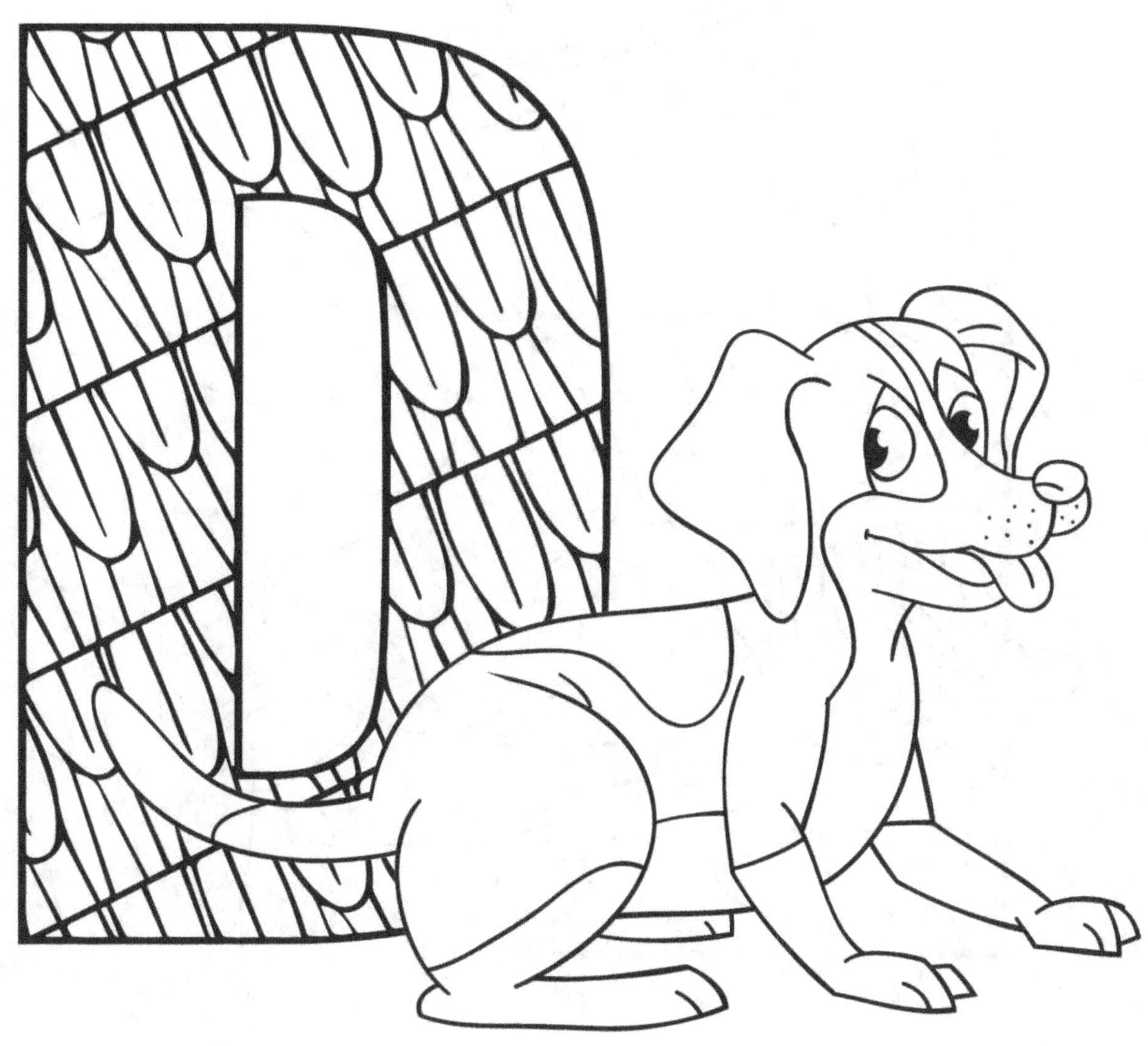

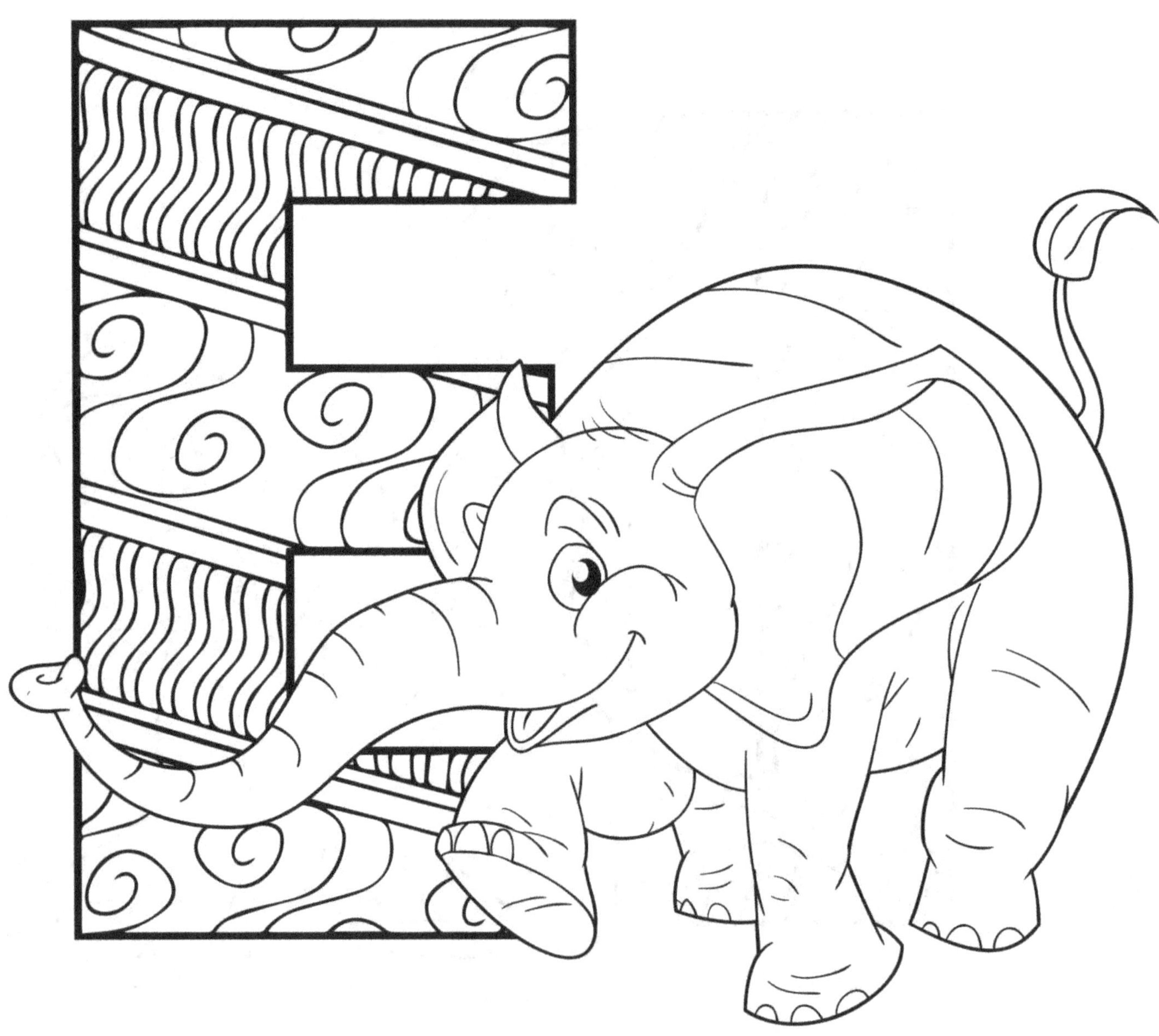

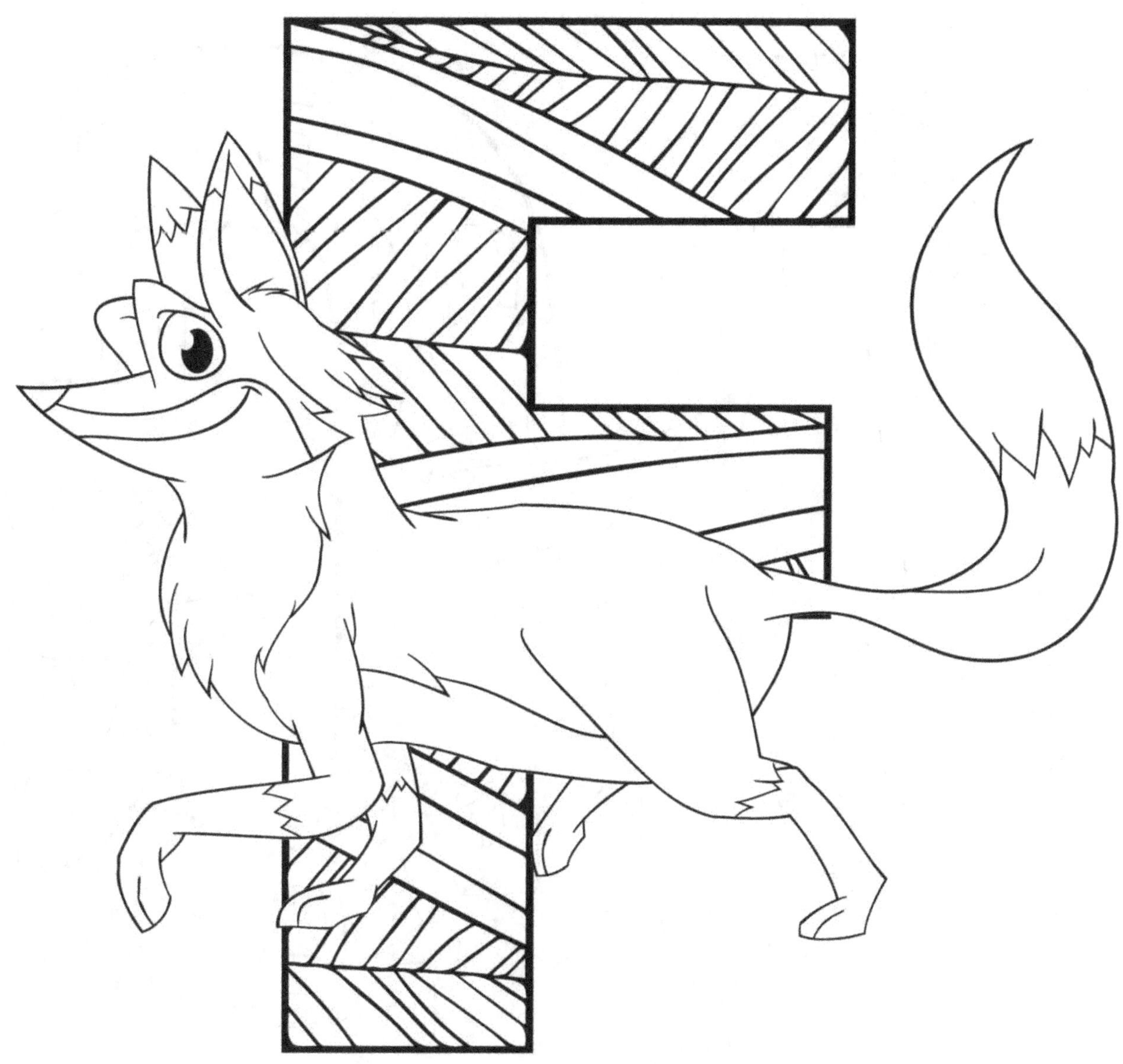

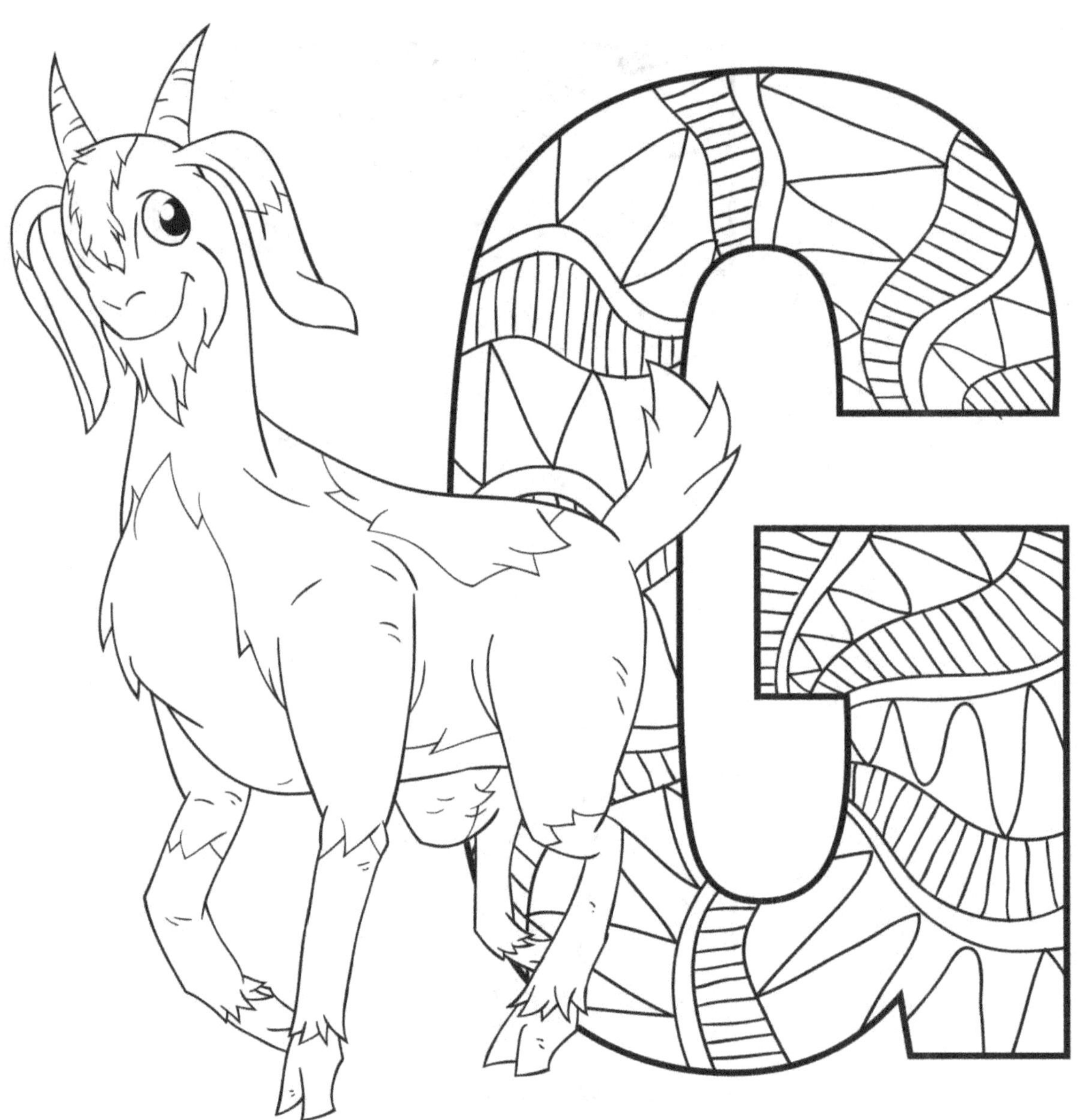

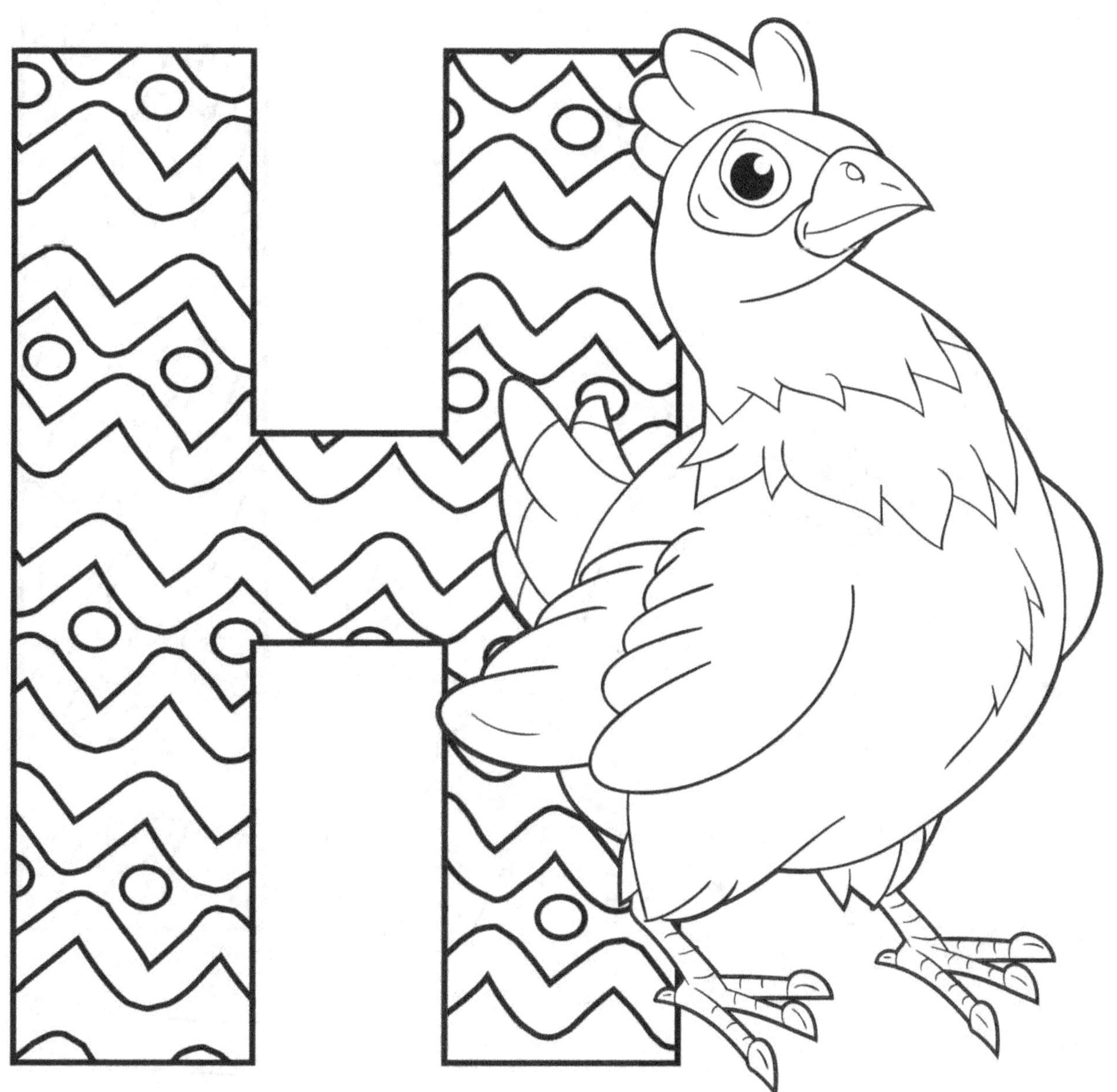

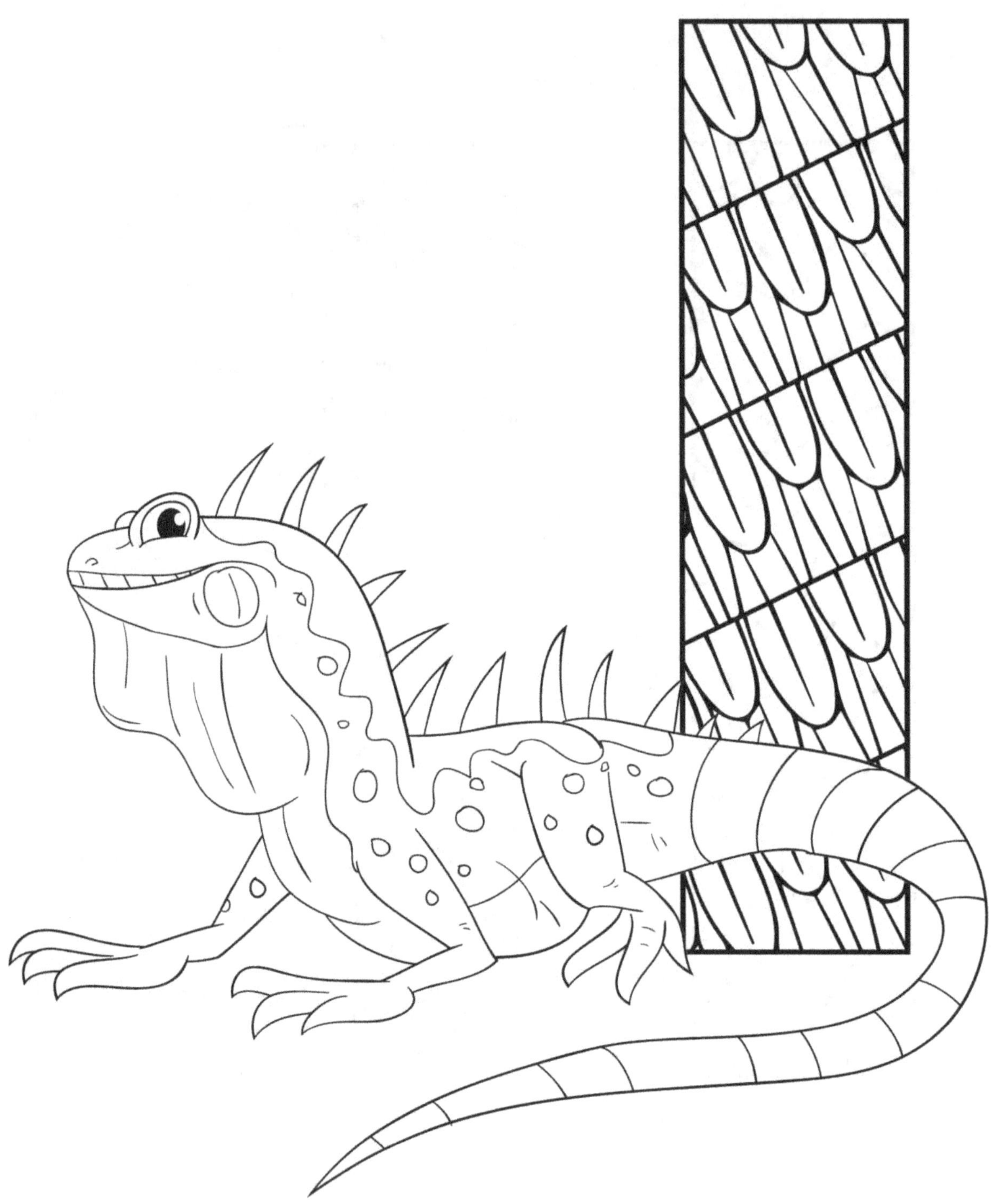

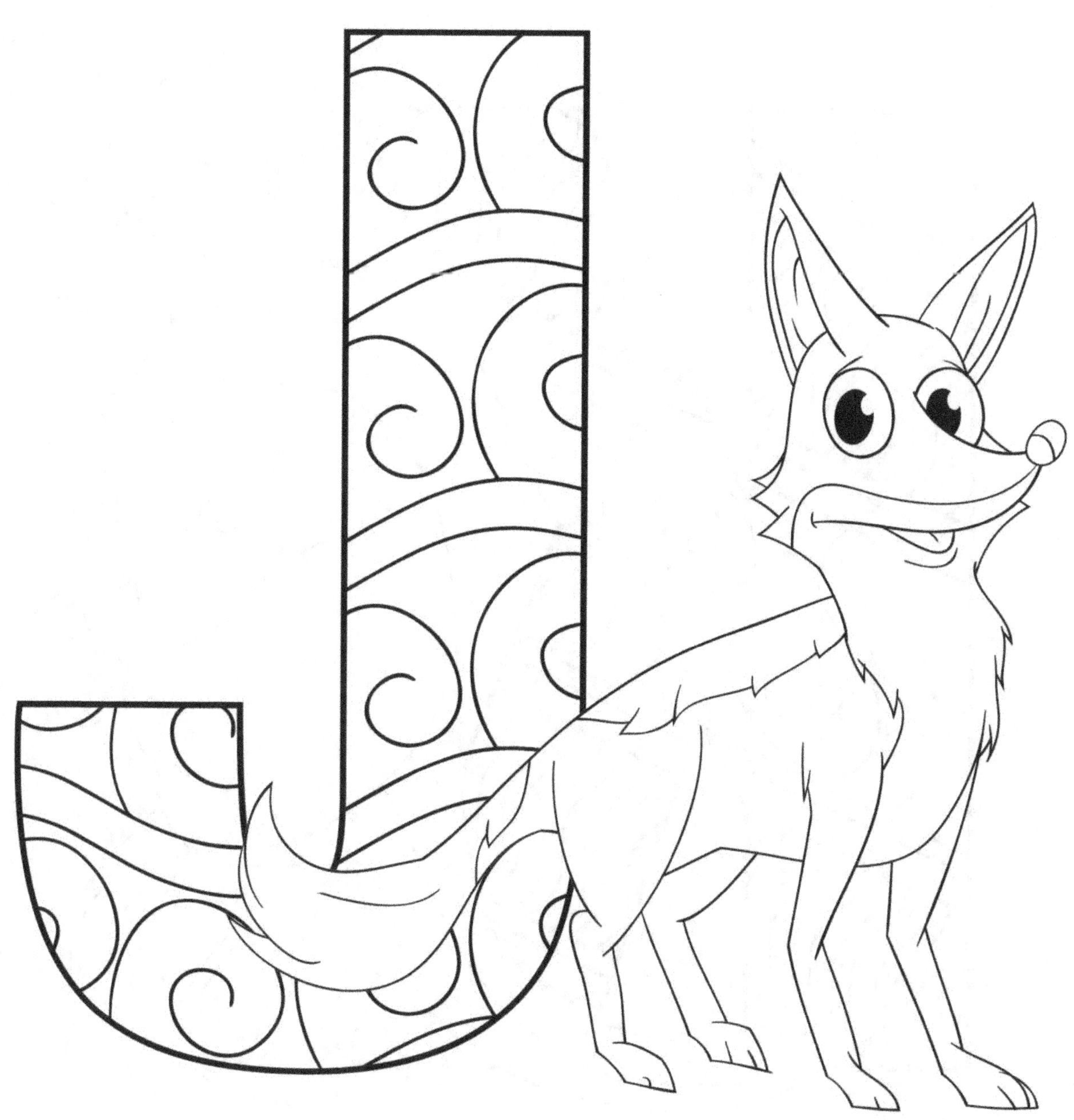

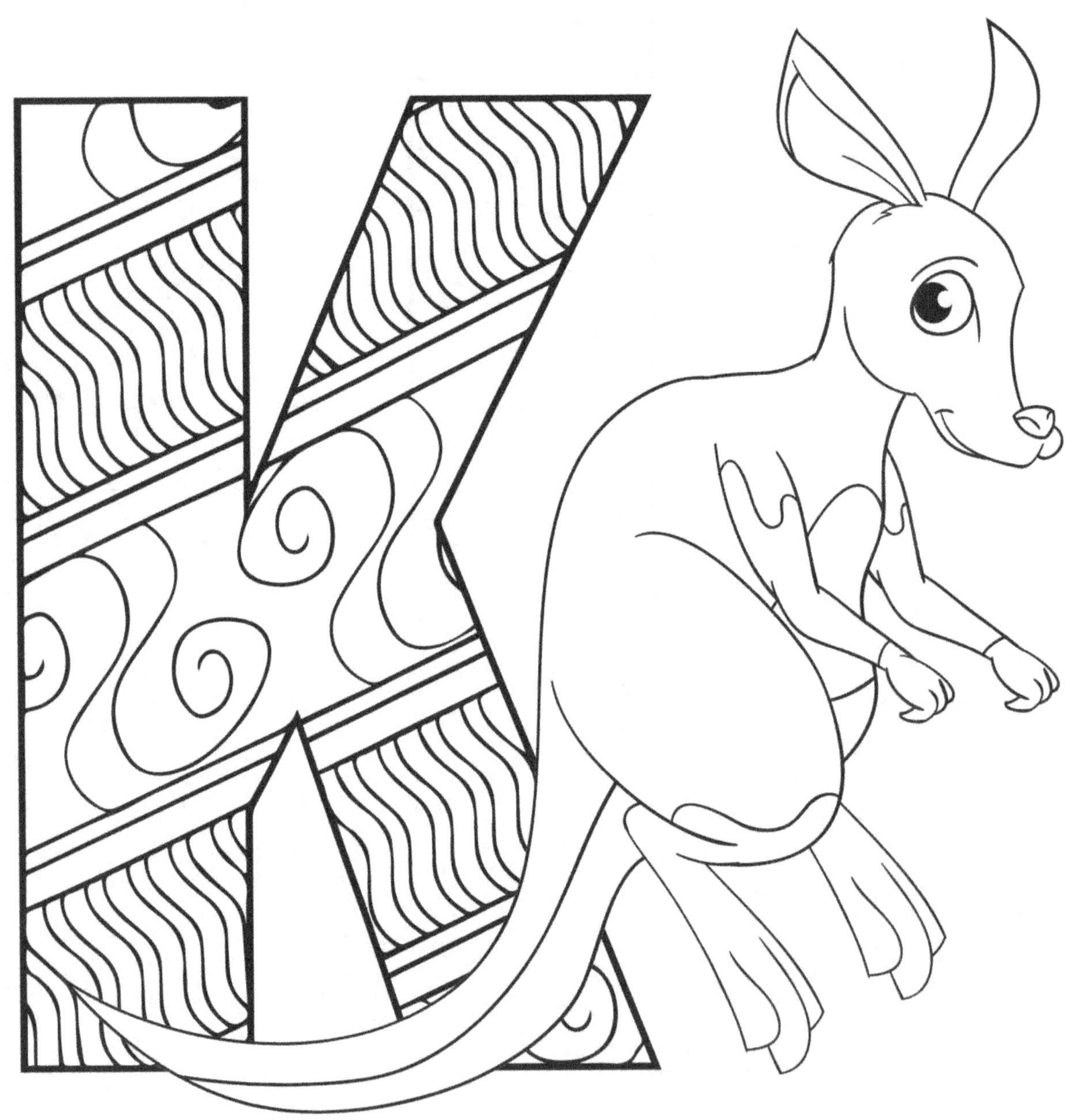

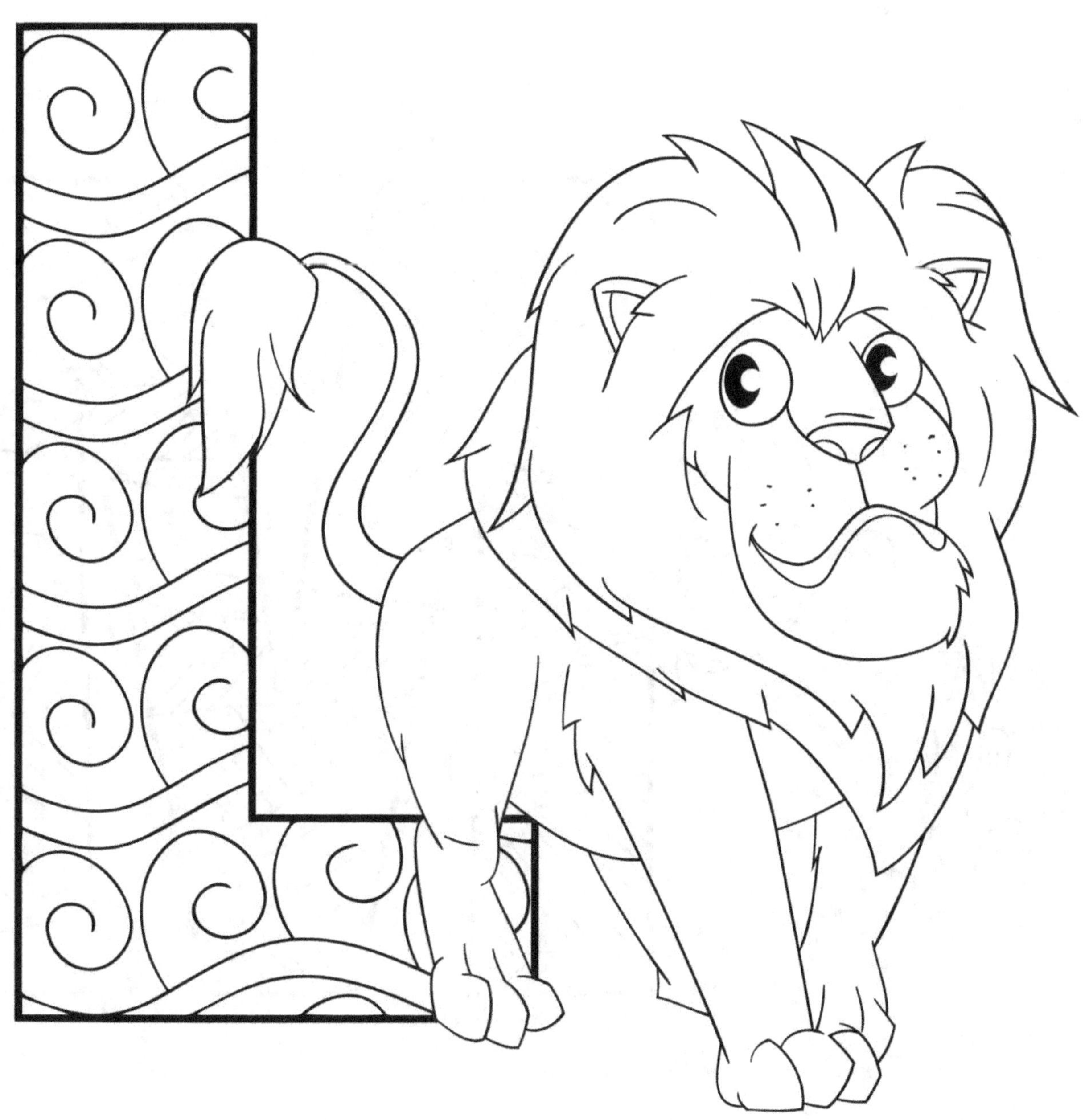

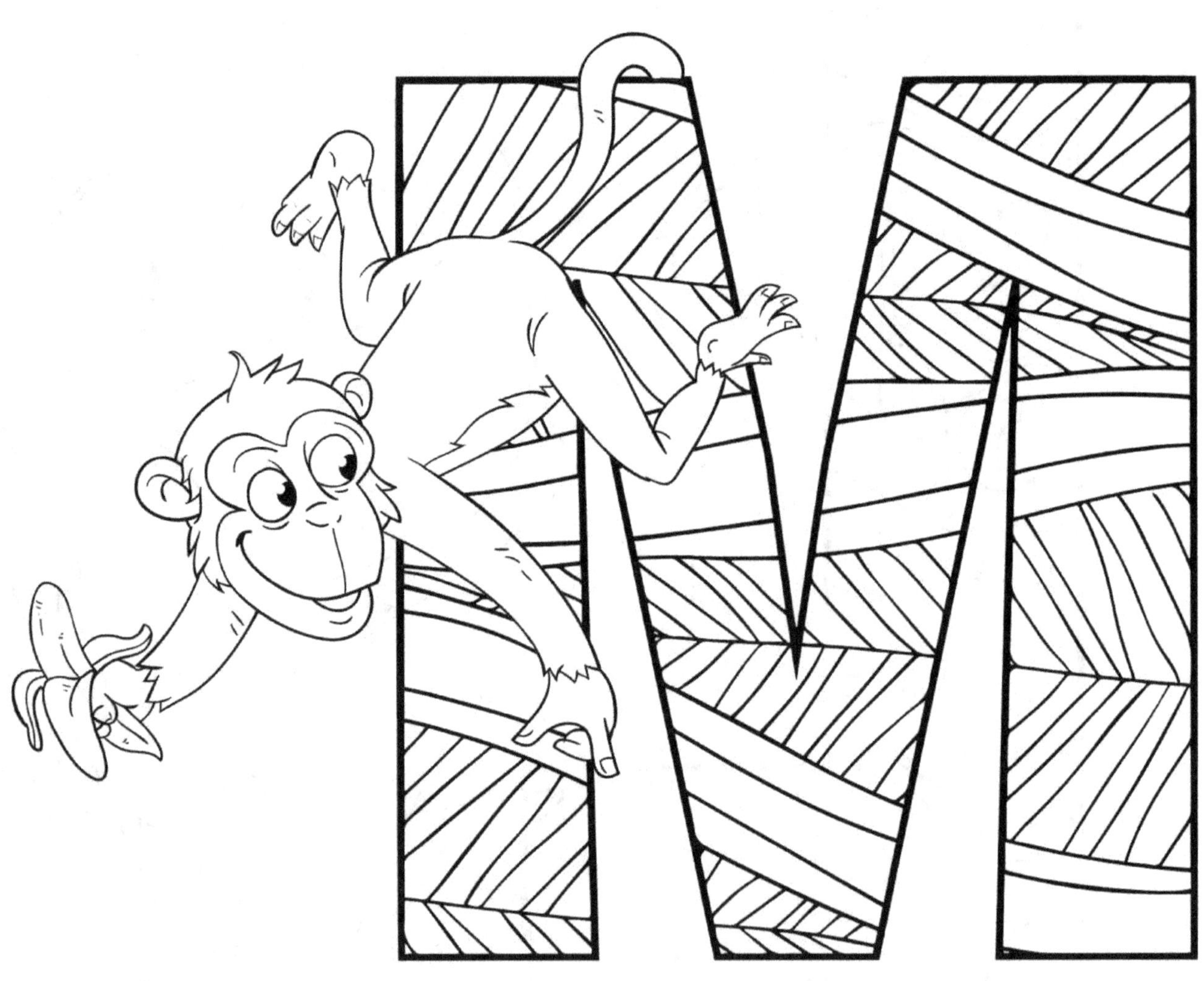

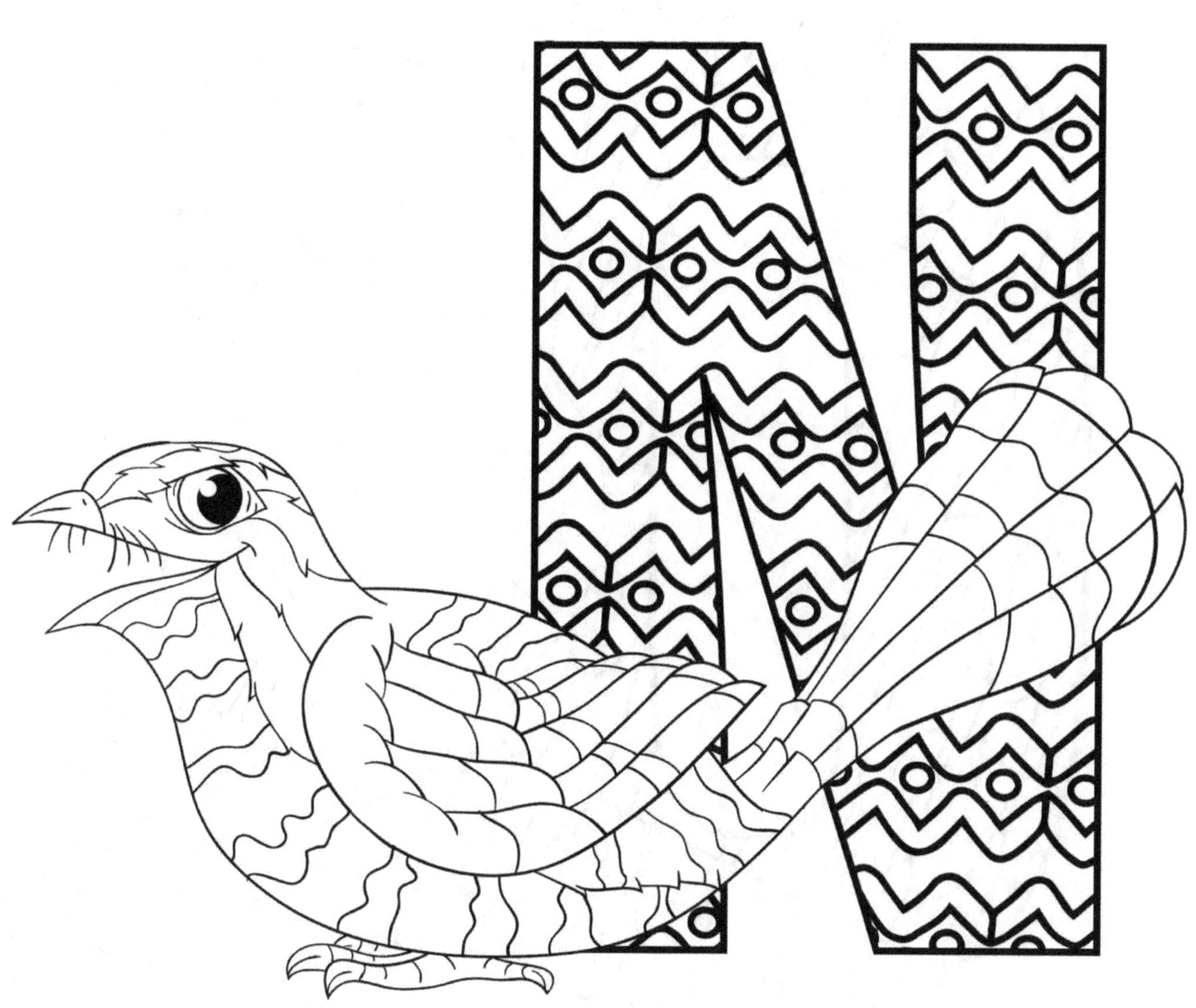

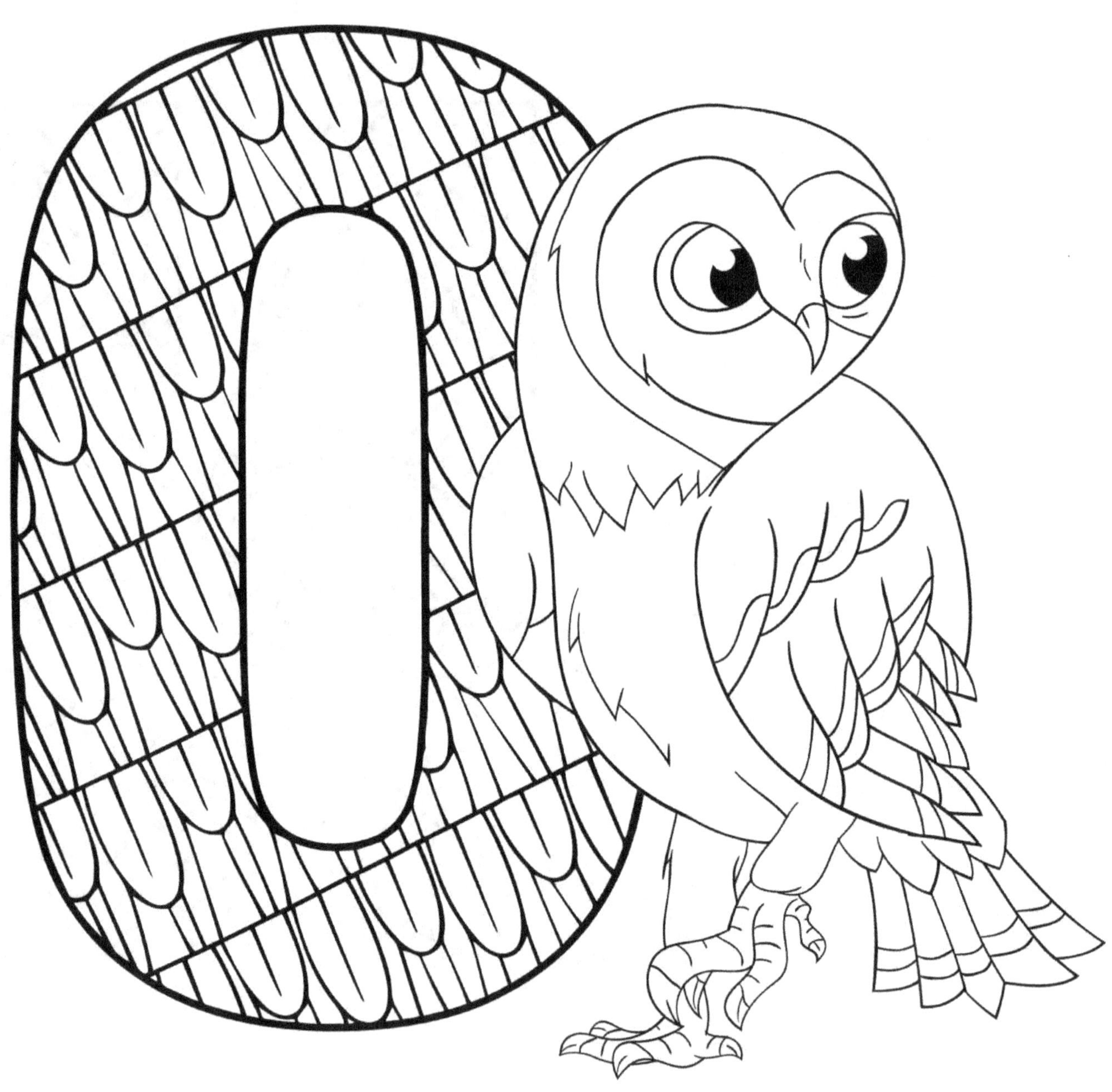

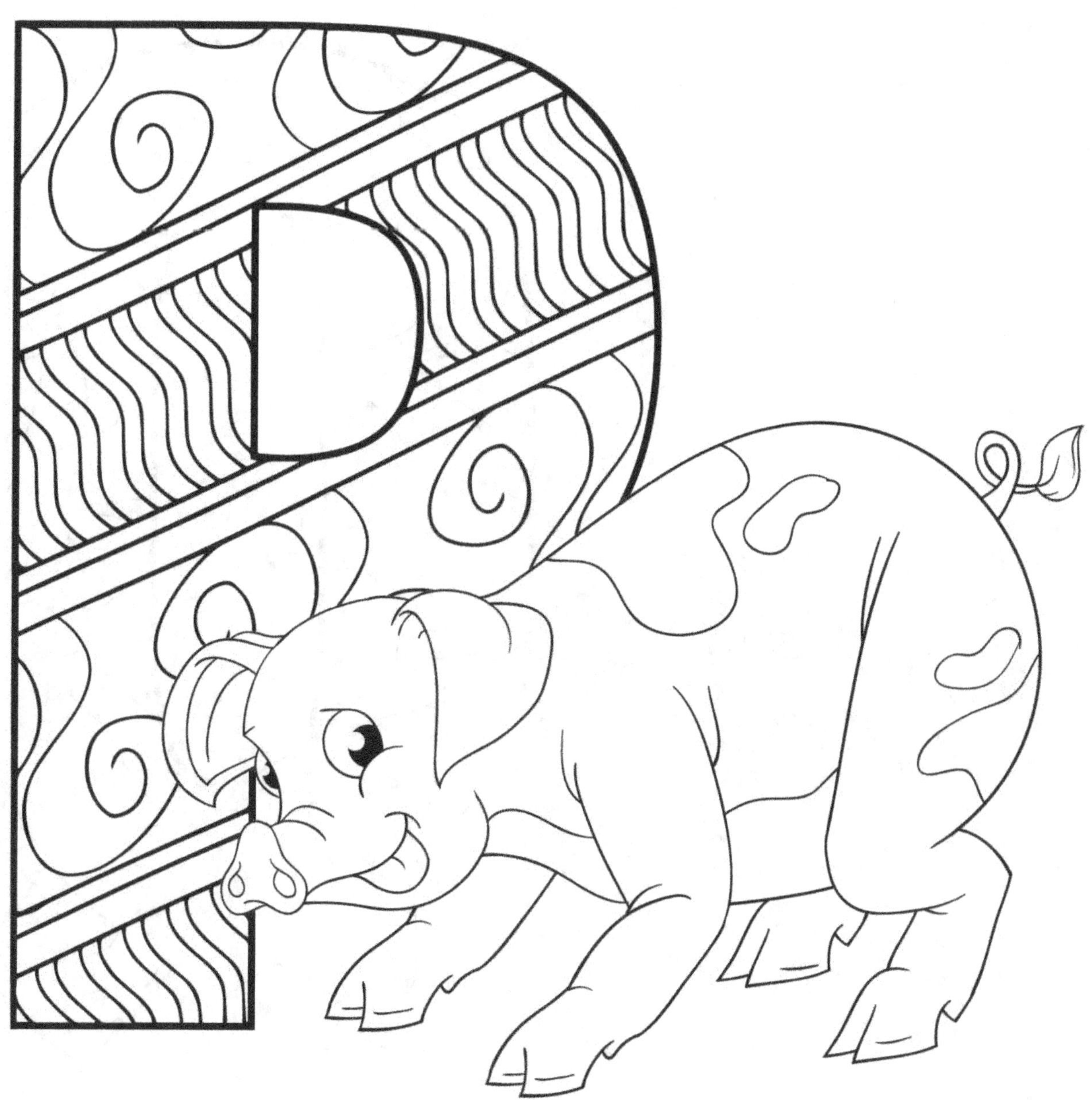

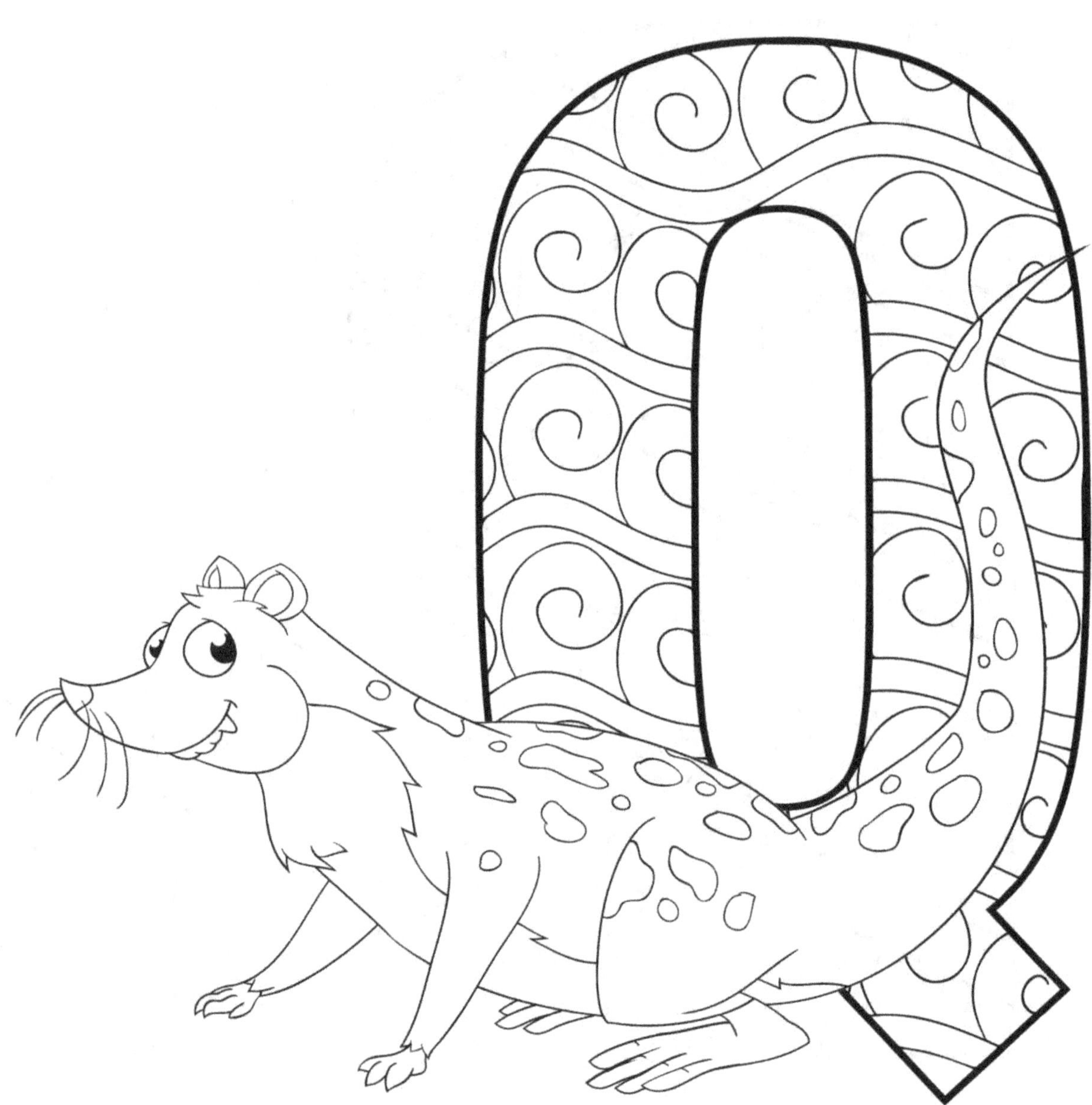

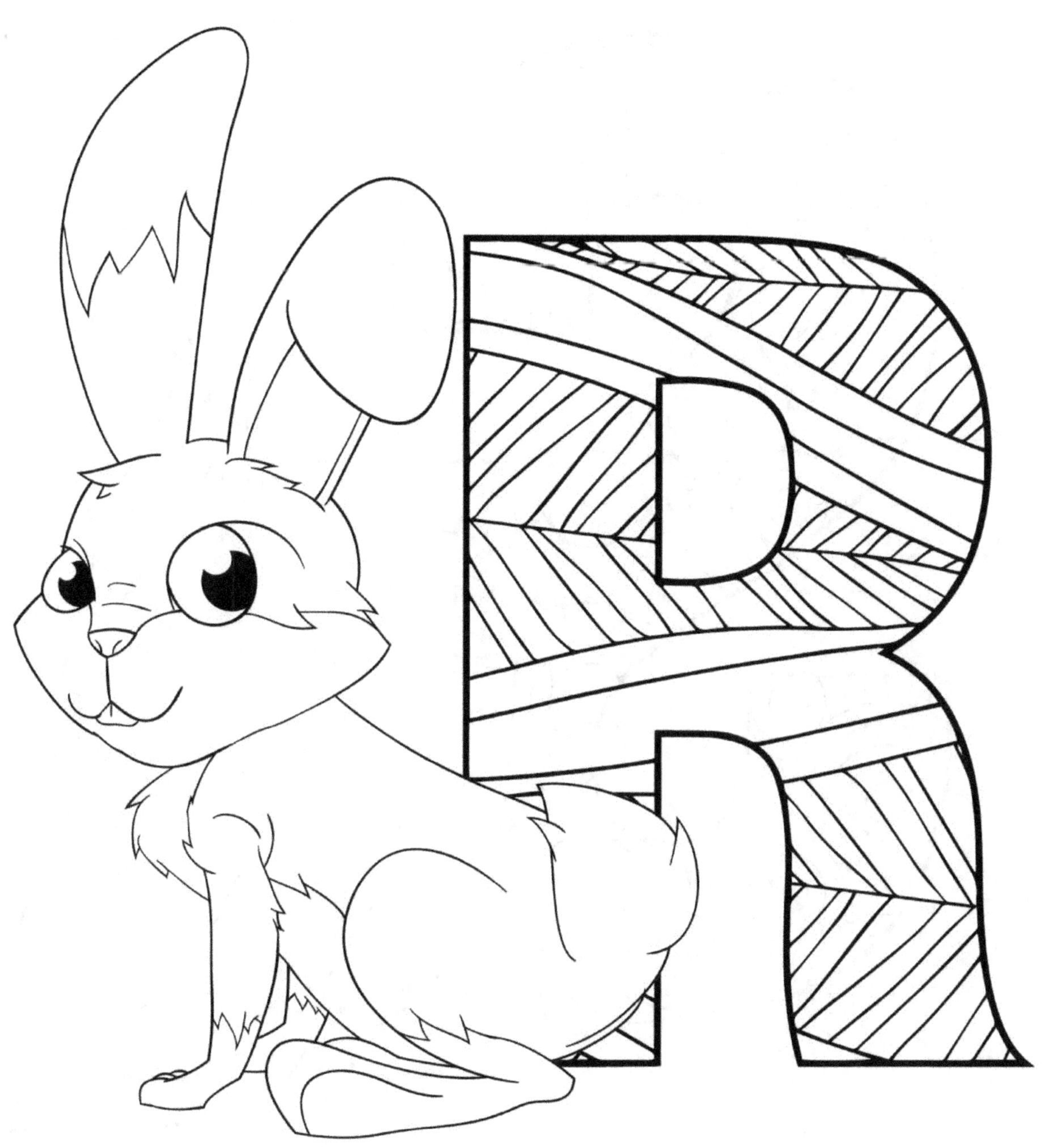

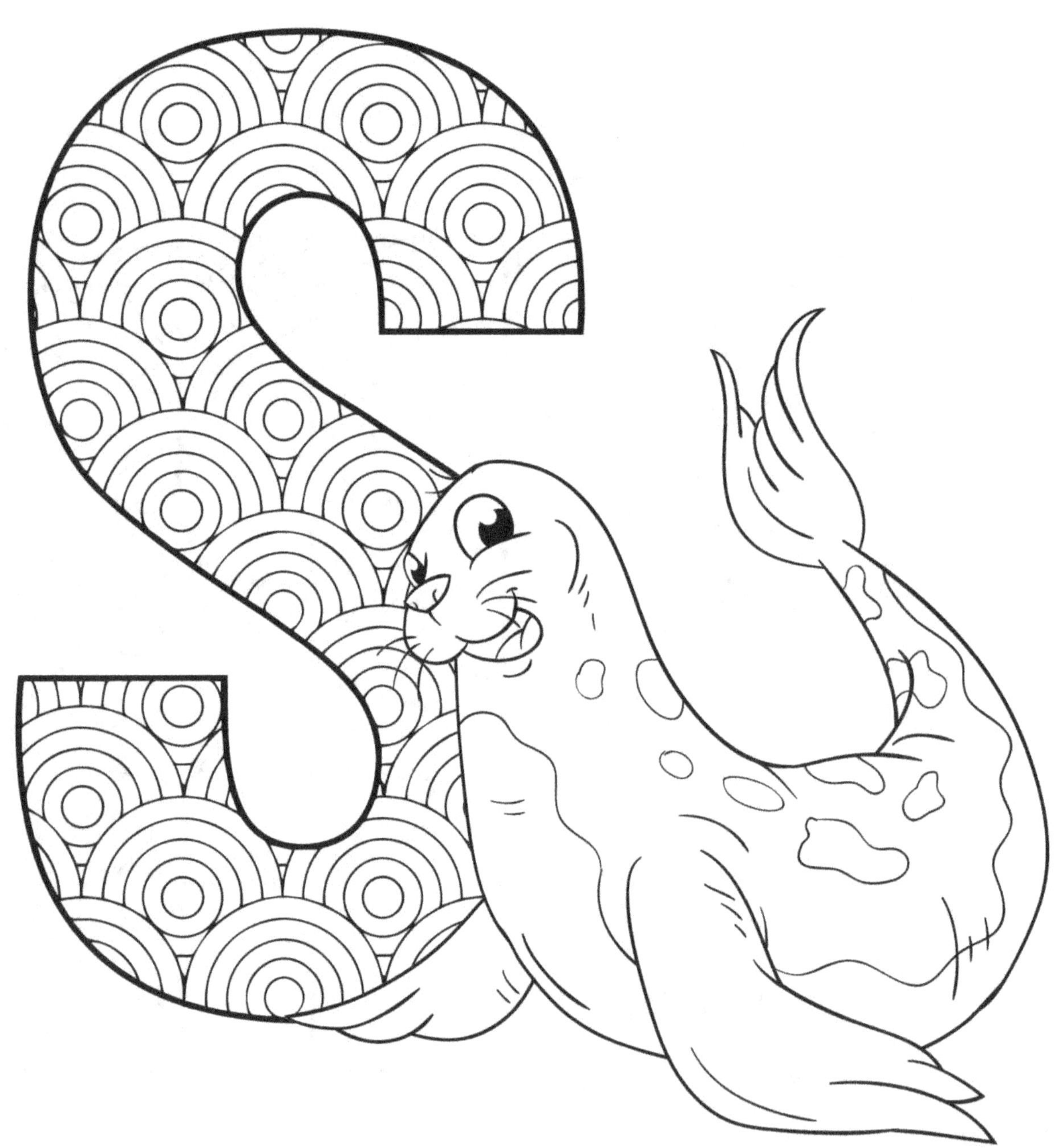

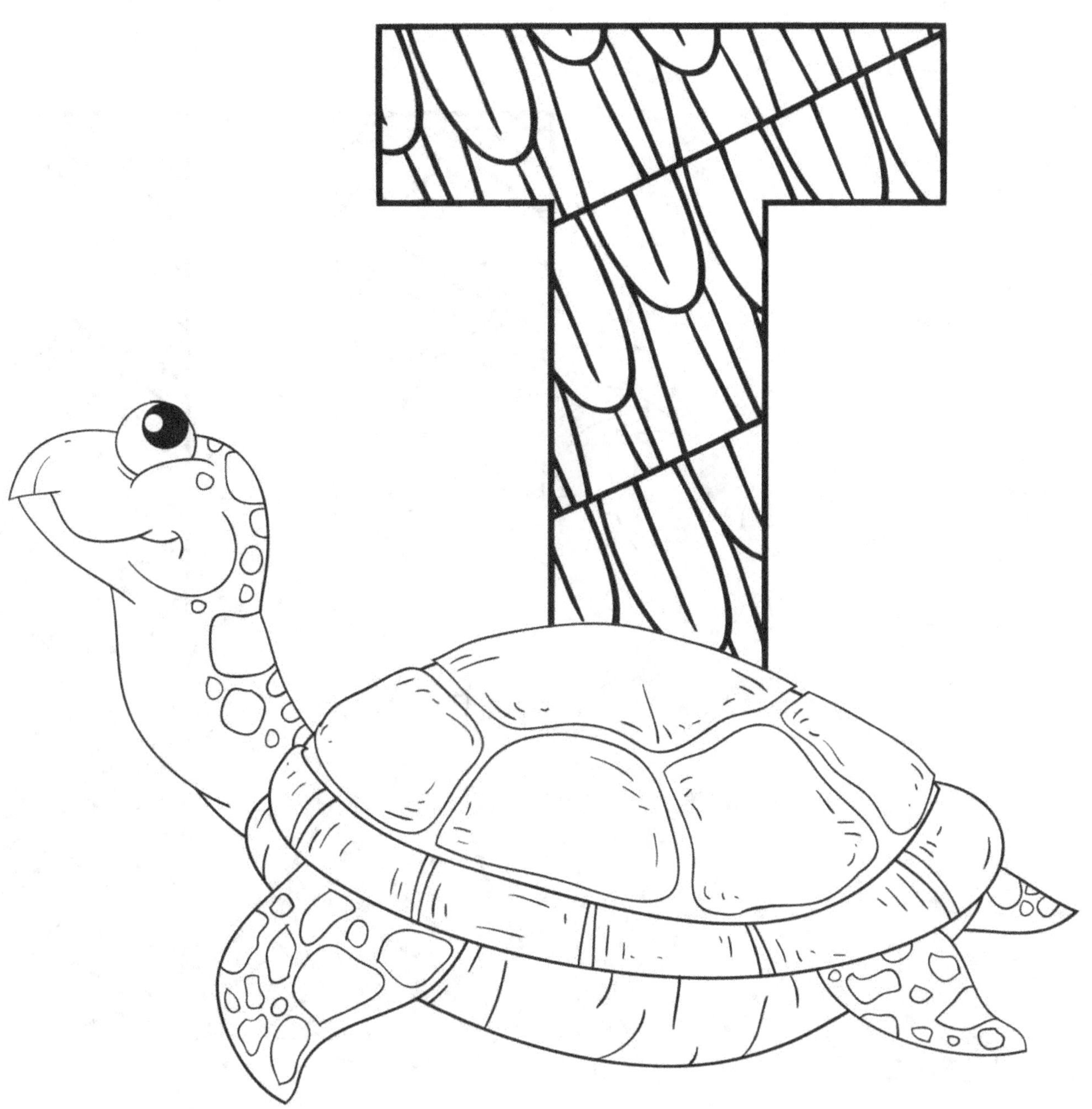

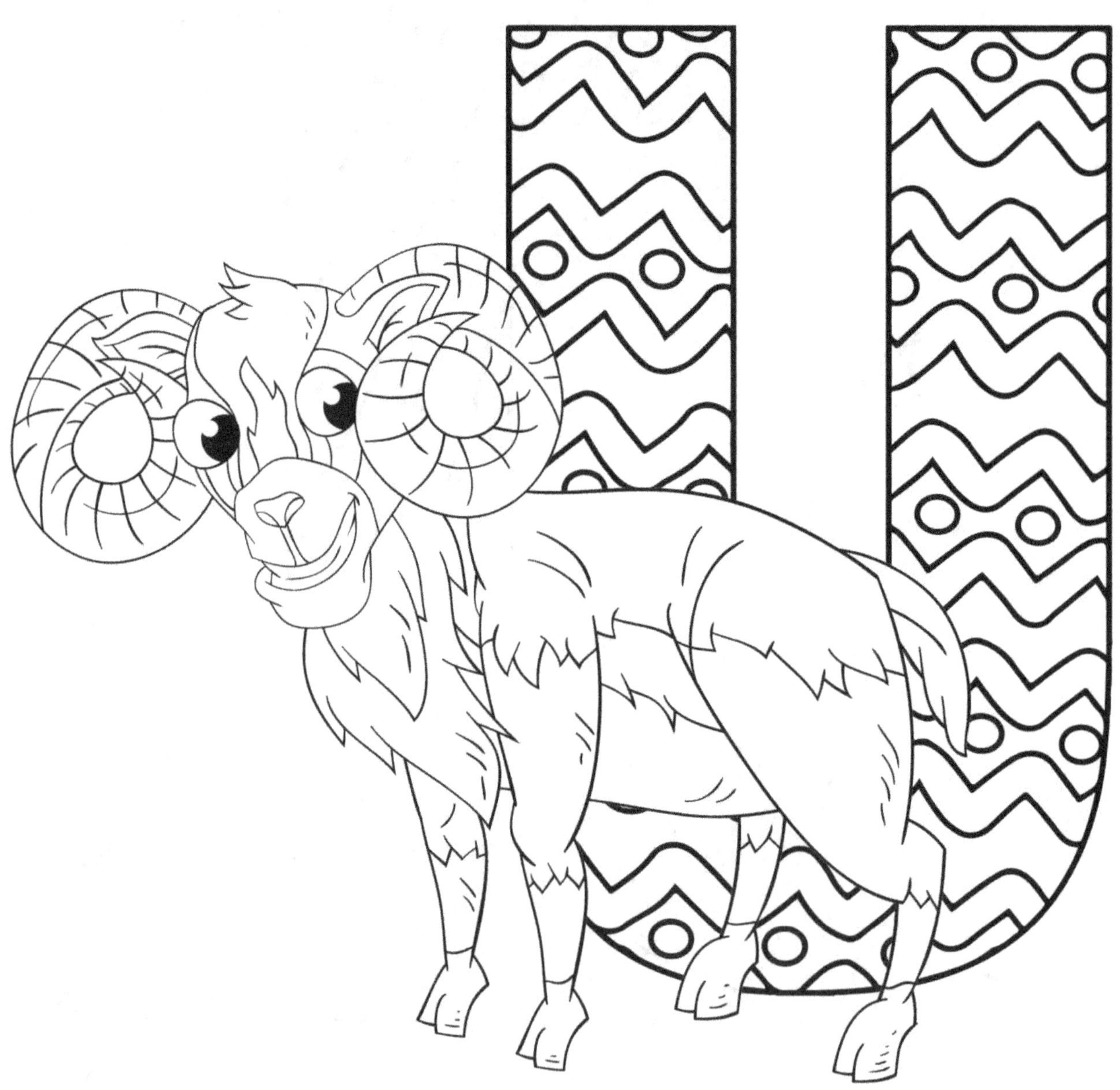

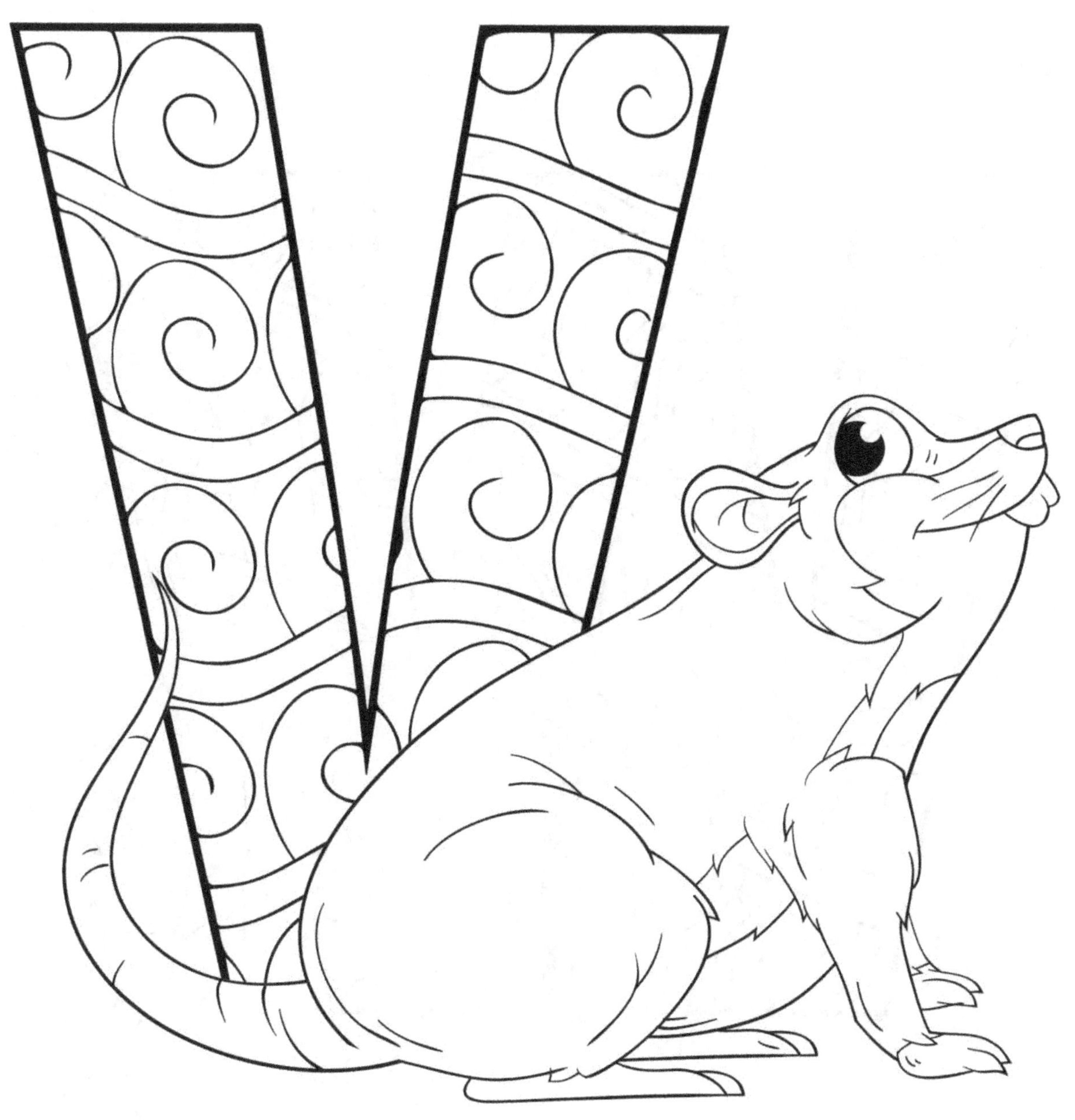

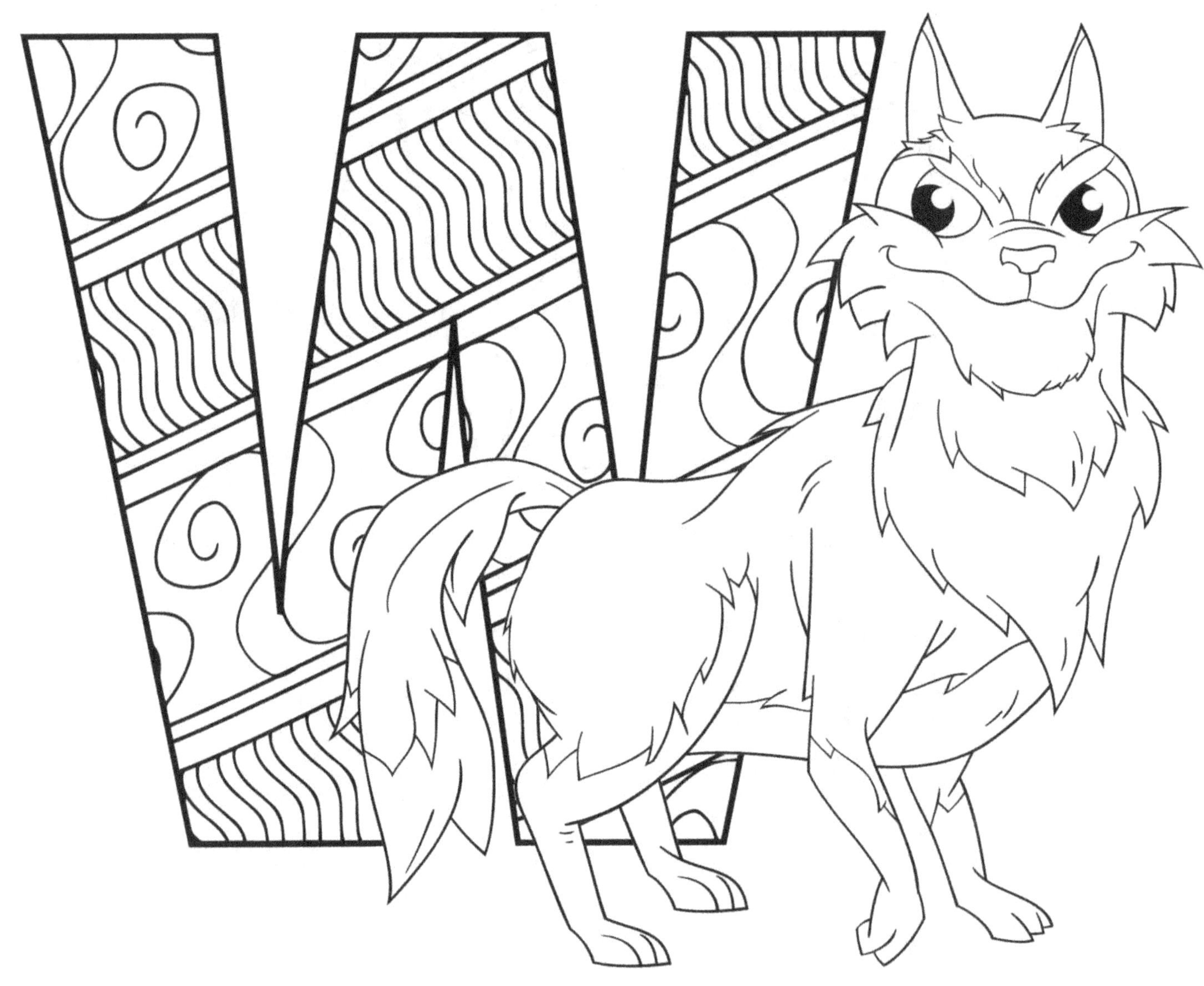

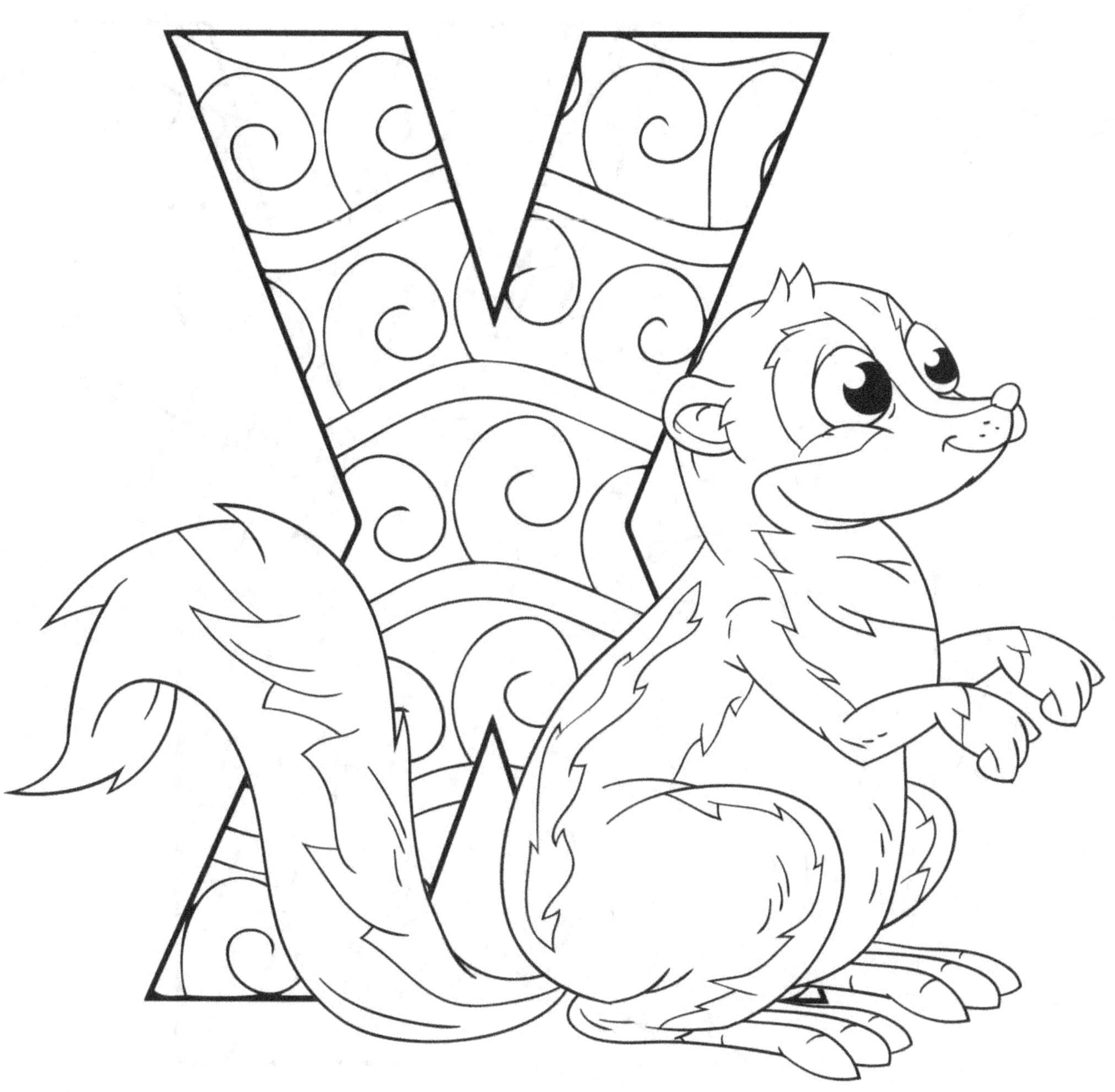

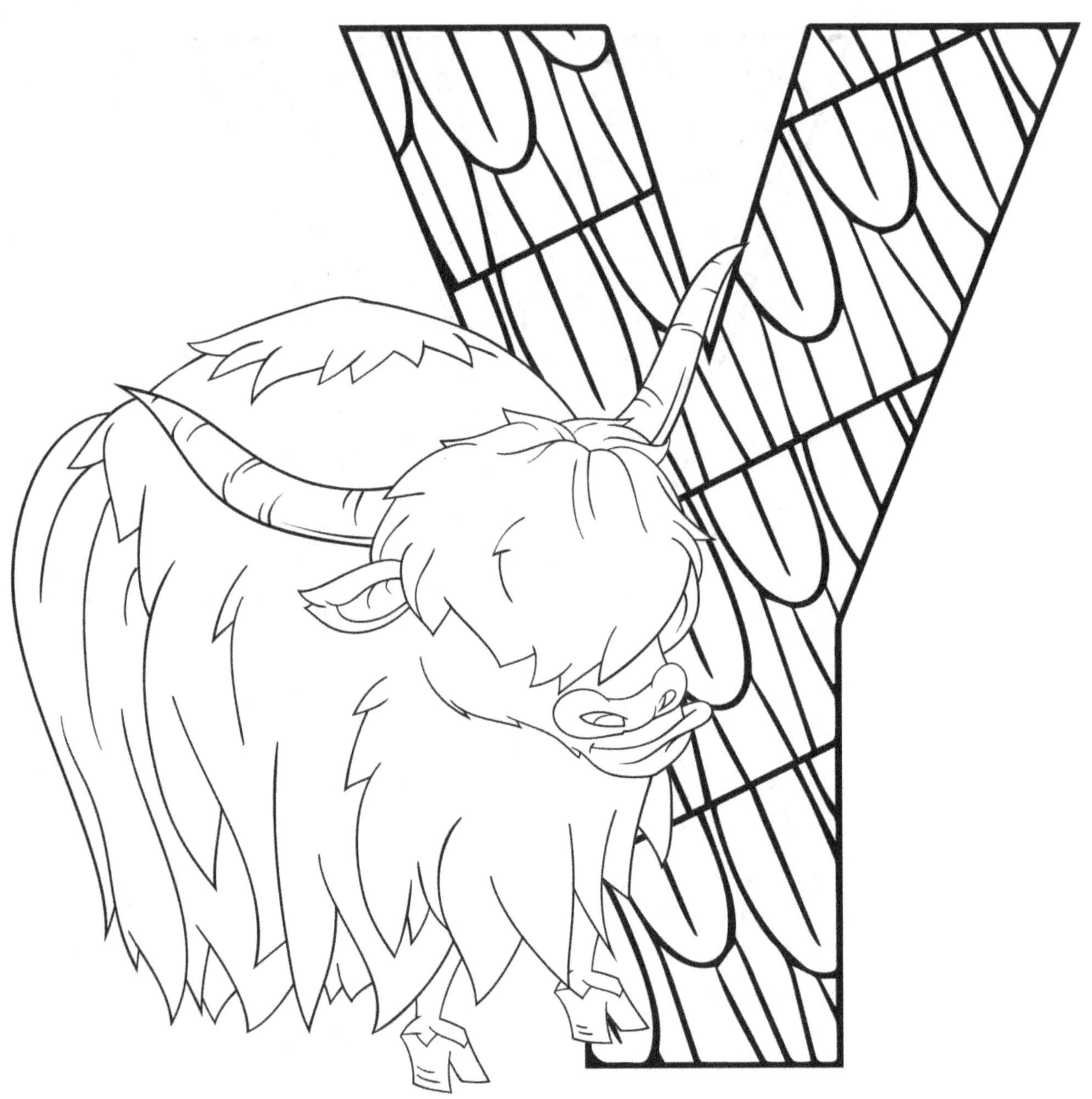

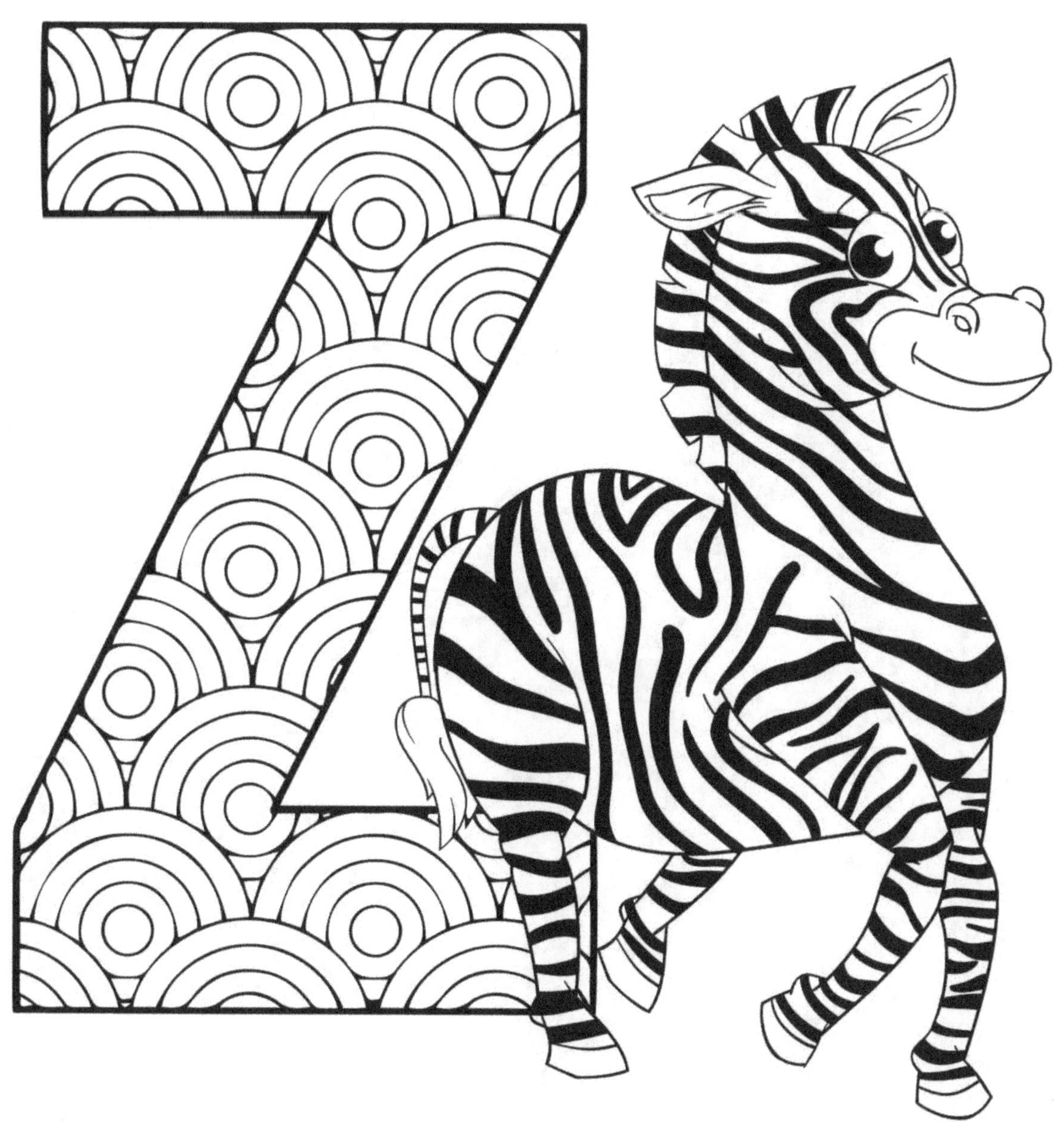